To

From

JOHN HADAMUSCIN'S

Simple
Pleasures

Also by John Hadamuscin

FROM MY HOUSE TO YOURS
Gifts, Recipes, and Remembrances
from the Hearth and Home

ENCHANTED EVENINGS
Dinners, Suppers, Picnics, and Parties

SPECIAL OCCASIONS
Holiday Entertaining All Year Round

THE HOLIDAYS
Elegant Entertaining from
Thanksgiving to Twelfth Night

JOHN HADAMUSCIN'S

Simple
Pleasures

101 Thoughts and Recipes for
Savoring the Little Things in Life

Photographs by Randy O'Rourke

HARMONY BOOKS / NEW YORK

Book design by Ken Sansone

Published by Harmony Books, a division of Crown Publishers, Inc.
201 East 50th Street, New York, New York 10022.
Member of the Crown Publishing Group.
Harmony and colophon are trademarks of Crown Publishers, Inc.
Manufactured in Japan

LIBRARY OF CONGRESS CATALOGING-IN-PUBLICATION DATA
Hadamuscin, John.
{Simple Pleasures}
John Hadamuscin's simple pleasures:
101 thoughts and recipes for savoring the little things in life/
photographs by Randy O'Rourke.
p. cm.
1. Cookery. I. Title. II. Title: Simple pleasures
TX652. H316   1992
641.5—dc20   92-7506 CIP

ISBN 0-517-59081-6

10 9 8 7 6 5 4 3 2 1
FIRST EDITION

"Let your boat of life be light,
packed with only what
you need—a homely home
and simple pleasures..."

JEROME K. JEROME

"The shortest pleasures
are the sweetest."

FARQUAHR

FOREWORD

Early one morning last summer I took my coffee out onto the terrace as I usually do during the warmer months. As I looked out toward the little white birdhouse down the hill, I spotted a vivid blue morning glory, the first one to blossom amidst the tangle of vines and leaves that for weeks had been reaching up the pole. And suddenly I realized I was smiling. Now there wasn't anything unusual there. Oh, I knew that in only a few more mornings the pole would be covered with a far more eye-popping array of bright blooms. But it was that one single flower, the first to appear on a plant that sprouted up from a few seeds I had poked into the ground only a few weeks before, that gave me that little thrill.

The thrill needn't always be a surprise like that first morning glory was. I get the same kind of pleasure when I encounter the first snow of the season, even if the weatherman's already given me fair warning. Or when I get a whiff of a pie I've just taken from the oven that's cooling on the windowsill. Maybe these little joys have something to do with reminding us of the past or reaffirming the continuity of life—or maybe they just plain bring us back down to earth—but many of them are the things that we all seem to share.

From the time we were small kids, my parents encouraged my brothers, my sister, and me to take pleasure in those sweet and simple moments that can pop up on any old day, those moments that are sometimes spontaneous, and never overly orchestrated. And as I've gotten older, and life continues to become more complicated and complex, I suppose I'm just like everyone else—those simple things, those simple pleasures, continue to be what often make us most happy. When I think of Peter Pan asking the Darling children to think lovely thoughts so they can fly, there's still something to be said about that simple one-word answer: "Candy!" It's the little things in life that we all long to return to; these are the things that make us fly.

So here are a few thoughts, a few pictures, and even a few recipes for some of my own simple pleasures, and I'd guess, some of yours, too. And if something here sparks off a memory of a simple pleasure or two of your own, all the better.

John

Cookies and milk

CRANBERRY OATMEAL COOKIES

Oatmeal cookies are the universal comfort food — in the morning, during the afternoon, or just before bed.

2 cups firmly packed light
    brown sugar
1 cup (2 sticks) butter
2 large eggs
1½ teaspoons vanilla extract
3 cups quick-cooking oats
1½ cups all-purpose flour
1 teaspoon baking soda

2 teaspoons ground cinnamon
½ teaspoon ground cloves
½ teaspoon salt
1½ cups dried cranberries
    (raisins or chopped dates
    can be substituted)
1 teaspoon grated orange rind

1. Preheat the oven to 350°F. Lightly grease baking sheets.

2. In a large mixing bowl, cream together the brown sugar and butter, beat in the eggs and vanilla, and then beat in the oats. In a separate bowl, stir together the flour, baking soda, spices, and salt.

3. A third at a time, stir the flour mixture into the wet mixture until well blended, then stir in the dried cranberries and orange rind.

4. Drop the dough by rounded teaspoonfuls onto the prepared baking sheets, about 2 inches apart. Bake until the cookies are golden brown, 8 to 10 minutes. Remove to wire racks to cool, then store in tightly covered containers in a cool place.

Makes about 4 dozen

Rereading a favorite novel ～

Watching reruns of "I Love Lucy" ～

Hearing an old clock chime ～

Sitting by the fire

on a winter afternoon

&

Making New Year's resolutions

&

Breaking New Year's resolutions

&

Making hot chocolate

after coming in from the cold

〜

HONEST-TO-GOODNESS HOT CHOCOLATE

When I was a kid, nothing could beat the welcoming smell of hot chocolate after walking home from school on a cold day or coming inside from ice skating. Even now, it's still the best medicine for warming body and soul.

1 ½ cups boiling water
½ cup unsweetened cocoa
  powder
Pinch of salt
½ cup sugar
½ teaspoon ground cinnamon
6 cups milk
1 ½ teaspoons vanilla extract
6 to 8 large marshmallows
6 to 8 peppermint sticks

1. In a small, heavy saucepan stir together the water, cocoa, salt, sugar, and cinnamon. Place over low heat and bring to a simmer; continue simmering until the mixture is well blended and slightly syrupy, about 2 minutes. Remove from the heat and reserve.

2. In a separate pan, heat the milk over low heat until just below the simmering point. Remove the pan from the heat and stir in the cocoa syrup. Stir in the vanilla, cover, and let stand 5 minutes before serving.

3. Ladle the hot chocolate into mugs and add a marshmallow and a peppermint stick to each mug.

Serves 6 to 8

*Meat loaf
and mashed potatoes
for supper*

MUSHROOM MEAT LOAF

Even when I get bored with other foods, I never tire of the comfort that meat loaf and mashed potatoes always seem to offer.

1 pound lean ground beef
1 pound ground turkey
1 cup finely chopped
    mushrooms (about 6 ounces)
2 large eggs
½ cup quick-cooking oats
¾ cup chopped parsley
1 medium onion, finely chopped
½ teaspoon dried sage
½ teaspoon dried thyme
½ teaspoon freshly ground
    black pepper

1. Preheat the oven to 350°F.

Have ready a shallow, rectangular baking dish or pan.

2. In a large mixing bowl, combine all the ingredients. Using your hands, mix until the ingredients are just blended. Turn the mixture out onto a clean work surface and shape it into a rectangular loaf about 9 x 5 inches.

3. Place the loaf in the pan and place in the oven. Bake until the loaf is firm and well browned, about 1 ¼ hours, basting occasionally with the pan juices. Remove from the oven and allow to stand 10 to 15 minutes before slicing. Serve with mushroom gravy.

Serves 6 to 8

MUSHROOM GRAVY

3 tablespoons butter
1 small garlic clove, finely
    chopped
1 small onion, finely chopped
1 cup thinly sliced mushrooms
    (about 6 ounces)
2 medium shiitake mushrooms,
    finely chopped
3 tablespoons flour
1 ½ cups beef stock
Pinch of grated nutmeg
Salt and freshly ground black
    pepper to taste

1. In a medium, heavy saucepan, combine the butter, garlic,
onion, and mushrooms. Place
over medium-low heat and
sauté until the onion is
softened and golden,
about 10 minutes.

2. Gradually stir in the flour,
continuing to stir until well
blended. Turn the heat up to
medium-high, then gradually
pour in the beef stock, stirring
constantly with a wire whisk.
Bring the mixture to a simmer
and return the heat to medium-
low. Simmer, stirring constantly, until the mixture is smooth
and thickened, 5 to 7 minutes.
Season to taste with nutmeg,
salt, and pepper and serve hot.

*Makes about
2 cups*

*A bunch of daisies
on the kitchen table*

Tomato soup and toasted cheese sandwiches

TOMATO AND RED PEPPER SOUP

Once I invited friends over for tomato soup and sandwiches — they thought I was kidding. Well, they're still my friends and this is still one of my spur-of-the-moment standbys for an evening in front of the television or the fireplace.

3 tablespoons butter
1 medium onion, coarsely chopped
1 large garlic clove, chopped
½ cup coarsely chopped celery
3 tablespoons flour
1 quart low-fat milk
3 cups tomato puree
4 red bell peppers, roasted, peeled, and seeded
Salt and freshly ground black pepper to taste

1. In a medium, heavy saucepan combine the butter, onion, garlic, and celery. Place over medium heat and sauté until the vegetables are tender, about 10 minutes. With a slotted spoon transfer the vegetables to the bowl of a food processor fitted with the steel chopping blade; reserve.

2. Whisk the flour into the butter remaining in the pan and continue whisking until completely blended in. Very gradually whisk in the milk; continue cooking on medium heat, whisking constantly, until the mixture thickens. Gradually stir in the tomato puree, whisking constantly. Bring the mixture to just below the simmering point, remove from the heat, and cover.

3. Add the red peppers to the food processor, along with a few tablespoons of the saucepan mixture, and process until smooth. Stir this mixture into the saucepan, return to medium heat, and cook, stirring constantly, until just below the simmering point. Season to taste with salt and pepper and serve.

Serves 4 to 6

TOASTED CHEESE SANDWICHES

Swiss cheese with ham and
   horseradish mustard on
   rye bread
Sharp Cheddar and bacon with
   chopped mango chutney
   on pumpernickel bread
Smoked mozzarella with red
   pepper and thinly sliced red
   onion on sourdough bread
Brie with smoked turkey breast,
   chopped scallions, and honey
   mustard on whole wheat
   bread

Taking an afternoon nap

*B*uilding
a snowman
〜

*M*aking a wish
〜

Receiving a secret Valentine

❧

Slipping under the bedcovers on a cold night

❧

Ice skating

❧

Cinnamon doughnuts for breakfast

CINNAMON-CHOCOLATE CHIP DOUGHNUTS

These are perfect for dunking into strong coffee or hot chocolate while daydreaming at the kitchen window.

2 ½ cups all-purpose flour
1 tablespoon baking powder
½ teaspoon salt
4 teaspoons ground cinnamon
½ teaspoon grated nutmeg
½ cup granulated sugar
1 large egg
½ cup milk
2 tablespoons vegetable short-
    ening, melted and cooled
¾ cup chocolate chips
Vegetable oil, for frying
¼ cup confectioners' sugar

1. In a mixing bowl, sift together the flour, baking powder, salt, 3 teaspoons of the cinnamon, and the nutmeg. In a separate bowl, lightly beat together the sugar, egg, and milk, and then beat in the shortening. Fold the wet mixture into the dry mixture until just blended, then stir in the chocolate chips.

2. On a floured surface, pat out the dough to a circle ½ inch thick. Cut out the dough with a doughnut cutter and reserve.

3. Pour vegetable oil into a large heavy pot or Dutch oven fitted with frying or candy thermometer to a depth of 1 ½ inches. Place over medium-high heat until the oil reaches 365°F. Fry the doughnuts in a single layer until golden brown on both sides, about 7 minutes. Remove to absorbent paper to drain off excess fat and cool.

4. In a small brown paper bag, combine the remaining cinnamon and the confectioners' sugar. One or two at a time, shake the doughnuts in the sugar mixture to coat.

Makes 10 to 12, depending on the size of the cutter

Playing cards with old friends

on a rainy day

Browsing through gardening catalogs

on a cold winter night

A *new puppy*

⌘

*D*aydreaming when there's work to be done

⌘

A *baby's smile*

⌘

Taking your shoes off

Watching
   for the first flowers
      that push through the ground

Curling up
   with the Sunday papers

Whistling a happy tune

~

*Forcing blossoms
from branches
before spring*

~

*The first whiff of coffee
in the morning*

~

SPICY PEACH COFFEE CAKE

Here's the perfect eye-opener on a lazy morning: a cup of just-brewed coffee and a slice of this spice-scented coffee cake.

½ cup sugar
⅓ cup (⅔ stick) butter, softened
1 large egg, lightly beaten
1 teaspoon vanilla extract
1 cup sifted all-purpose flour
1 teaspoon baking soda
¼ teaspoon salt
1 teaspoon ground cinnamon
1 teaspoon ground ginger
½ teaspoon grated nutmeg
½ teaspoon ground cardamom
3 firm ripe peaches, peeled and diced
½ cup chopped pecans, toasted

TOPPING
½ cup firmly packed dark brown sugar
2 tablespoons all-purpose flour
2 teaspoons ground cinnamon
1 teaspoon ground ginger
2 tablespoons (¼ stick) butter, melted
½ cup chopped pecans

1. Preheat the oven to 350°F. Lightly grease a 9-inch square cake pan.

2. In a mixing bowl, cream together the sugar and butter, then beat in the egg and vanilla. In a separate bowl, sift together the flour, baking soda, salt, and spices. Add the dry mixture to the wet mixture and stir until just blended. Stir in the peaches and pecans. Transfer the batter to the prepared pan.

3. To make the topping, combine all the ingredients in a small bowl and mix to form coarse crumbs. Sprinkle this mixture over the cake batter and bake until a tester comes out clean, about 45 minutes. Cool in the pan on a wire rack. Serve warm or at room temperature, cut into squares.

Makes one 9-inch square cake

The first barbecue of the year

RHUBARB BARBECUE SAUCE

Come spring, two of the things I look forward to most are rhubarb and the season's first barbecue. What's better than two favorite things except maybe two favorite things combined?

1 medium orange, unpeeled, seeded, and finely chopped
2 tablespoons coarsely chopped gingerroot
1 large garlic clove, coarsely chopped
¾ cup cider vinegar
½ cup water
1 ½ cups coarsely chopped rhubarb
2 cups firmly packed light brown sugar
½ teaspooon salt
⅛ teaspoon cayenne pepper

1. In a medium, heavy, non-reactive saucepan, combine the orange, ginger, garlic, vinegar and water. Place over medium-high heat and bring to a boil. Reduce the heat to low, cover loosely, and simmer 15 minutes. Add the rhubarb, brown sugar, and salt and continue simmering until the mixture has thickened, about 20 minutes longer. Stir in the cayenne pepper; add a bit more if you like it hotter.

2. Transfer the mixture to the bowl of a food processor fitted with the steel chopping blade and pulse-process until the mixture is a slightly lumpy puree. Store in jars in the refrigerator.

3. Brush the sauce liberally on almost-cooked grilled chicken, duck, pork chops, or ribs. Serve more sauce at the table.

Makes about 3 cups

*Seeing the first robin
of spring*

❧

The sound of rain on the roof

❧

*The smell of lilacs
through an open
window*

❧

*Watching a butterfly dance
through the garden*

Lending a hand to a friend

Riding a bicycle

Blowing bubbles

⌒

Looking for the Big Dipper
on a crystal-clear night

⌒

Watching a skywriter

⌒

P*icking strawberries*

∽

HOMEMADE STRAWBERRY SHORTCAKE

Every summer when we were kids we'd go with Mom to a local berry farm and pick baskets and baskets of strawberries. We'd eat strawberries every which way, but this is still my favorite.

1 ½ pints strawberries, washed, hulled, and halved
3 tablespoons sugar

SHORTCAKES
⅞ cup all-purpose flour
1 ½ teaspoons sugar
1 ½ teaspoons baking powder
¼ teaspoon salt
2 tablespoons (¼ stick) cold butter
⅜ cup milk

1 cup heavy cream
Pinch of salt
1 teaspoon sugar
2 to 3 tablespoons butter, softened

1. Combine the strawberries and 3 tablespoons sugar in a bowl, toss well, cover, and refrigerate.

2. To make the shortcakes, preheat the oven to 425°F. Lightly grease a baking sheet. In a large mixing bowl, combine the flour, sugar, baking powder, and salt, then cut in the butter. Stir in the milk and mix until the dry ingredients are just moistened. Do not overmix.

3. On a well-floured work surface, lightly pat out the dough to a thickness of ⅜ inch. Using a 3-inch round biscuit cutter, cut out circles of dough and transfer them to the prepared baking sheet. Bake until the shortcakes are lightly browned, 12 to 15 minutes. Transfer to a wire rack to cool.

4. To assemble the shortcakes, beat the cream until soft peaks form and then beat in the salt and sugar. Split the shortcakes in half and butter them lightly. Place the bottom halves in individual serving dishes and spoon the berries over them. Top with whipped cream and the tops of the shortcakes. Serve immediately with soupspoons.

Serves 6

Watching a sailboat glide by

The
smell of tea roses
in bloom

❧

Listening to children at play

❧

The smell of fresh air-dried bedsheets

❧

Lemonade on the lawn

RASPBERRY LEMONADE

On a hot and muggy summer afternoon, nothing satisfies like a frosty glass of pink lemonade.

2 quarts water
1 ½ cups sugar
½ pint raspberries
Juice of 10 lemons
1 lemon, thinly sliced

1. In a heavy, nonreactive saucepan, combine the water, sugar, and raspberries. Place over medium heat and bring to a boil, stirring until the sugar is dissolved. Reduce the heat and simmer for 10 minutes. Remove from the heat and allow to cool to room temperature.

2. Strain the raspberry syrup mixture into a pitcher, add the lemon juice and lemon slices, and chill. Serve the lemonade over ice in tall glasses.

Makes about 2 quarts

*Working in
the garden*

~

Watching the breeze rustle the curtains

~

Lying in a hammock under a shady tree

Sitting on a screened-in porch
during a summer thunderstorm

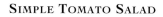

Picking the summer's
first tomato

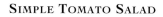

SIMPLE TOMATO SALAD

A perfect, sun-ripened,
just-picked tomato needs little
adornment, and this simple
salad lets the tomato shine.

4 large, ripe, unrefrigerated
   tomatoes, cut into wedges
3 tablespoons extra-virgin
   olive oil
2 teaspoons balsamic
   vinegar
1 small sweet onion, very
   thinly sliced

2 teaspoons fresh oregano leaves
   or ½ teaspoon dried oregano,
   crumbled
Generous pinch of salt
Plenty of freshly ground black
   pepper

Combine all ingredients in a
small bowl, toss well to combine, cover, and let stand 1
hour. Serve immediately.

Lunch for 2

Flying a kite

❧

Sleeping under the stars

❧

Raiding the refrigerator for a midnight snack

❧

Watching fireflies blinking across the yard

❧

The smell of just-cut grass

❧

Going fishing

PAN-FRIED
CATCH OF THE DAY

This is my favorite way
of fixing fresh-caught fish,
learned from my father,
"the great fisherman."

1 cup rolled oats
¼ teaspoon salt
¼ teaspoon freshly
   ground black pepper
¼ teaspoon paprika
2 tablespoons very finely
   chopped parsley
¼ cup milk
2 large eggs, lightly beaten
2 pounds firm white fish fillets
Vegetable oil, for frying
Lemon wedges

1. In a shallow bowl, combine
the oats, salt, pepper, paprika,
and parsley. In a separate bowl,
combine the milk and eggs. One
at a time, dip the fish fillets first
into the milk mixture, then into
the oatmeal mixture, turning to
coat both sides well. Wrap the
fillets loosely in wax paper and
refrigerate for 10 minutes.

2. Pour vegetable oil into a large
skillet to a depth of about ¼
inch, place over medium-high
heat, and heat the oil until it
sizzles, about 350°F. Add the
fish to the skillet in one layer
(fry in batches or 2 skillets if
necessary) and fry about 3 minutes on each side, or until the
fish is firm and the coating is
golden brown. Serve hot with
lemon wedges.

Serves 6

A *picnic in the park*

PICNIC POTATO SALAD

Picnics and potato salad —
you can't have one without
the other.

½ cup white wine vinegar
½ cup olive oil
1 teaspoon Dijon mustard
1 small garlic clove,
   finely chopped
½ teaspoon salt
¼ teaspoon freshly ground
   black pepper
1 teaspoon sugar

3 pounds red new potatoes,
   unpeeled, cooked, drained,
   and quartered
½ head cauliflower flowerets,
   steamed crisp-tender
1 bunch broccoli flowerets,
   steamed crisp-tender
½ pound snowpeas, cut
   diagonally in half and
   steamed crisp-tender
½ cup diced celery
1 medium red onion, sliced
   and separated into rings
1 medium red bell pepper, diced
½ cup chopped parsley

1. In the bottom of a large mixing bowl, combine the vinegar,
oil, mustard, garlic, salt, pepper,
and sugar; whisk to blend. Add
the potatoes while still hot and
toss to coat well with the dress-
ing. Add the remaining ingredients and toss to combine.

2. Cover and refrigerate; return
to room temperature before
serving.

Serves 8 to 10

*P*laying

horseshoes

∽

*W*atching *a small-town parade*

∽

*C*anoeing *on a lake*

∽

Building a sand castle

Fitting into last year's clothes

Ice cream on a hot summer night

BLUEBERRY-BUTTERMILK ICE CREAM

On hot summer nights, Mom and Dad would pile us into the car and off we'd go for a ride to cool off. Those rides would always include a stop for ice cream. Nowadays I make the ice cream myself in my air-conditioned kitchen, but it's still a great summer cooler.

2 pints blueberries
½ cup honey
1 tablespoon lemon juice
⅛ teaspoon ground cloves
½ cup sugar
¼ teaspoon salt
1 quart buttermilk
4 large egg yolks, lightly beaten
2 pints light cream or half-and-half
1 tablespoon vanilla extract

1. Combine the blueberries, honey, lemon juice, and cloves in a small heavy saucepan and place over medium heat. Bring the mixture to a boil, reduce heat to low, and simmer for 5 minutes. Remove from the heat and cool.

2. In a separate pan, combine the sugar, salt, and buttermilk and bring to the scalding point, stirring to dissolve the sugar. Remove from the heat and slowly stir this mixture into a bowl containing the beaten egg yolks, stirring constantly until blended.

3. Pour the mixture back into the pan and return to the heat. Cook, stirring constantly, until the mixture thickens slightly, but do not allow the custard to boil. Remove from heat, stir in the cream and vanilla, and cool. Cover and chill thoroughly.

4. Stir the blueberry mixture into the custard mixture. Pour into an ice cream maker and freeze according to the manufacturer's directions.

Makes about 2½ quarts

*W*atching the Fourth of July fireworks

∽

*F*lower boxes
at the window

∽

Watching a Little League ball game

～

Morning glories

～

Riding down a river in an old inner tube

～

Thinking of things to make with all the zucchini in the garden

CAROLYN'S CHOCOLATE ZUCCHINI CAKE

Whenever I'm overwhelmed by zucchini and more zucchini, I call my friend Carolyn Spainhour, the zucchini expert, who always bails me out with a new idea. Well, she's done it again.

3 cups all-purpose flour
½ cup unsweetened cocoa
1 teaspoon baking soda
½ teaspoon baking powder
1 teaspoon ground cinnamon
1 teaspoon salt
1½ cups vegetable oil
3 cups granulated sugar
4 large eggs

1 teaspoon vanilla extract
3 cups grated unpeeled zucchini
Confectioners' sugar, for dusting

1. Preheat the oven to 350°F. Lightly grease a 10-inch tube pan or Bundt pan and dust it very lightly with cocoa.

2. In a mixing bowl, sift together the flour, cocoa, baking soda, baking powder, cinnamon, and salt. In a separate large bowl, combine the oil and granulated sugar, and then beat in the eggs, one at a time. A third at a time, beat the dry mixture into the wet mixture until well blended. Beat in the vanilla and then stir in the zucchini.

3. Transfer the batter to the prepared pan and bake until the edges come away from the pan and a cake tester comes out clean, about 1 hour.

4. Cool the cake in the pan 10 minutes, remove the cake to a wire rack, and allow to cool completely. Then dust lightly with confectioners' sugar. Cover and refrigerate until serving. Serve with whipped cream or vanilla ice cream.

Makes one 10-inch tube cake

Telling ghost stories

Listening to crickets at night

A *moonlight walk on the beach*

❧

*L*istening *to the waves of the ocean*

❧

An apple pie cooling on the windowsill

SOUR CREAM APPLE PIE

We Ohio kids always learned early on about Johnny Apple-seed. Of course, his name be-came my childhood nickname, but I still love apples, especially in this fragrant and juicy pie.

Double crust for a 9-inch pie
¾ cup firmly packed light
    brown sugar
2 teaspoons ground cinnamon
¼ teaspoon salt
2 tablespoons all-purpose flour
1 cup sour cream
1 large egg, lightly beaten
½ teaspoon vanilla extract
1 teaspoon grated lemon rind
6 cups peeled and thinly sliced
    baking apples, such as Gran-
    ny Smith or Yellow Delicious

1. Preheat the oven to 400°F. Line a 9-inch pie pan with a single crust.

2. In a large mixing bowl stir together the brown sugar, cin-namon, salt, and flour. Add the sour cream, egg, and vanilla and blend well, then stir in the lemon rind. Add the apples and toss to coat well with the sour cream mixture.

3. Fill the prepared pie crust with the apple mixture and use the remaining crust to make a lattice top. Bake 15 minutes, reduce heat to 350°F., and con-tinue baking until the crust is well browned and the apples are tender, 30 to 35 minutes.

Makes one 9-inch pie

Sharing an old family recipe

~~~

GRANDMA STAPLETON'S SAUERKRAUT SOUP

This humble soup, an old-country recipe that my grandmother often made for both family and company alike, is cheap and easy to make, and over the years it's warmed many souls.

6 strips thickly sliced bacon, coarsely chopped
1 tablespoon butter
2 medium onions, coarsely chopped
1 large clove garlic, finely chopped
2 16-ounce cans cannellini (white kidney beans), drained and rinsed
3 carrots, peeled and diced
3 medium boiling potatoes, unpeeled and diced
1 16-ounce can sauerkraut, with its liquid
6 cups chicken stock
½ teaspoon dried thyme
¼ cup chopped parsley
Freshly ground black pepper

1. In a large, heavy saucepan, combine the bacon, butter, onions, and garlic. Place over medium heat and sauté until the bacon has rendered its fat and the onions are golden, about 10 minutes.

2. Add the cannellini, carrots, potatoes, sauerkraut, and stock and stir well. Turn the heat to high and bring the mixture to a simmer. Reduce the heat and simmer until the potatoes are tender, about 20 minutes. Stir in the thyme and parsley and pepper to taste. Simmer 5 minutes longer and serve hot with crusty rye or pumpernickel rolls.

Serves 6

*C*orn on the cob

*H*aving your back scratched

A warm fluffy towel

*R*aking leaves

Carving Hallowe'en pumpkins

An old-fashioned hayride

BAKED MACARONI AND CHEESE

Pasta, pasta, pasta! When was the last time you had good old, plain and simple, crusty-topped baked macaroni and cheese?

½ cup (1 stick) butter
4 tablespoons flour
3 cups milk
3 cups grated sharp Cheddar
⅓ cup grated Parmesan
1 teaspoon salt
½ teaspoon dry mustard
⅛ teaspoon cayenne pepper
1 pound elbow macaroni, cooked al dente and drained
½ cup fine dry bread crumbs

1. In a medium, heavy saucepan over medium heat, melt ⅓ cup (⅔ stick) of the butter, then stir in the flour. When all the flour is absorbed, gradually add the milk, stirring constantly. Continue cooking, stirring constantly, until the sauce is thickened, 4 to 5 minutes. Add the cheeses and continue stirring until they are blended in. Stir in the salt, mustard, and cayenne.

2. Preheat the oven to 350°F. In a large bowl, combine the cheese sauce and the macaroni. Lightly grease a shallow 3-quart casserole and transfer the macaroni mixture to it. Sprinkle the bread crumbs over the macaroni and dot with the remaining butter. Bake until well browned, 30 to 40 minutes, and serve.

Serves 6 to 8

Watching Fred and Ginger dance

Reminiscing with old friends

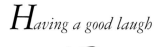

Having a good laugh

A hot fudge sundae

Taking a long hot bath

A *walk through the woods*
in October

Baking
a cake

~

OLD-FASHIONED SPICE CAKE

When I'm all wound up, nothing is more therapeutic than getting myself into the kitchen and baking a cake. And if the baking doesn't calm me down, the eating sure does.

⅔ cup (1⅓ sticks) butter, softened
2 cups firmly packed light brown sugar
4 large eggs
2 ⅔ cups all-purpose flour
1 teaspoon baking powder
1½ teaspoons baking soda
2 teaspoons ground cinnamon
1 teaspoon ground ginger
½ teaspoon grated nutmeg
½ teaspoon ground allspice
1⅓ cups buttermilk
1 teaspoon vanilla extract
1¼ cups raisins

FROSTING
1 cup firmly packed light brown sugar
¼ teaspoon cream of tartar
Pinch of salt
⅓ cup water
1 large egg white
½ teaspoon vanilla extract
½ cup shredded coconut, toasted
½ cup chopped walnuts, toasted

1. Preheat the oven to 350°F. Lightly grease two 9-inch round layer cake pans.

2. In a large mixing bowl, cream together the butter and brown sugar, then one at a time beat in the eggs. In a separate bowl, sift together the flour, baking powder, baking soda, and spices.

3. A third at a time, beat the dry mixture, alternating with the buttermilk, into the wet mixture, beating until smooth after each addition. Beat in the vanilla and then stir in the raisins.

4. Divide the dough between the two prepared pans and bake until the edges separate from the sides of the pan and a cake tester comes out clean, 25 to 30 minutes. Remove the cake layers from the pan to wire racks to cool.

5. To make the frosting, combine the brown sugar, cream of tartar, salt, and water in a small heavy saucepan over medium heat. Bring the mixture to a boil, then remove the pan from the heat. Slowly add the egg white, beating constantly with a rotary or electric beater. Continue beating until the mixture is fluffy and spreadable, then beat in the vanilla.

6. Frost the top of the bottom cake layer, add the top layer and frost the top and sides of the cake. Sprinkle the toasted coconut and walnuts over the top of the cake.

Makes one 9-inch layer cake

*S*topping for tea in

the afternoon

❦

SPICED TANGERINE TEA

Brewing and sipping a cup
of hot tea may be one of the
simplest pleasures of all.

4 tangerine slices
12 whole cloves
4 cinnamon sticks
2 tablespoons sugar
4 cups freshly brewed orange
    pekoe tea, brewed with the
    grated rind of 1 tangerine

Stud each tangerine slice with
3 cloves. Place a slice, a cinnamon stick, and 1 ½ teaspoons
sugar in each of 4 teacups. Fill
each cup with hot tea, stir with
the cinnamon stick, and serve.

Makes 4 servings

*R*eceiving a letter
from a faraway friend

❦

*W*indow-shopping

❦

*P*laying board games on
a cool fall night

∽

*L*istening to Nat King Cole
(or Ella, or Frank, or Judy, or. . .)

∽

*B*obbing for apples

∽

Sitting in an old rocking chair

Tapping your foot to a favorite tune

*Smelling the Thanksgiving turkey
as it roasts in the oven*

*Cooking Sunday supper
for friends*

GRANDMA WYNN'S CHICKEN PIE

Years ago this was a Sunday night specialty at my grandmother's house, and it's still a favorite at mine.

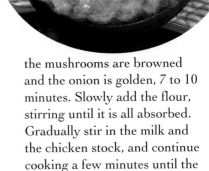

Double pastry crust for a
  9-inch pie
2 tablespoons (¼ stick) butter
1 cup sliced mushrooms
1 medium onion, chopped
3 tablespoons all-purpose flour
1 cup milk
1 cup chicken stock
4 cups cubed cooked chicken
1 cup fresh or frozen peas
1 cup sliced carrots
1 cup peeled pearl onions
¼ cup chopped parsley
2 teaspoons chopped tarragon
  or ½ teaspoon dried tarragon
Salt and freshly ground black
  pepper, to taste

1. Preheat the oven to 375°F. Line a 9-inch deep-dish pie pan with half the pastry dough.

2. In a large, heavy saucepan or Dutch oven over medium heat, combine the butter, mushrooms, and chopped onion. Sauté until the mushrooms are browned and the onion is golden, 7 to 10 minutes. Slowly add the flour, stirring until it is all absorbed. Gradually stir in the milk and the chicken stock, and continue cooking a few minutes until the sauce thickens.

3. Stir the chicken, peas, carrots, pearl onions, and herbs into the pan; season to taste with salt and pepper. Transfer to the prepared pan, top with the remaining crust, and crimp the edges. Cut a few slits into the top crust to allow steam to escape during baking. Bake until the crust is nicely browned, 40 to 45 minutes. Serve hot.

Serves 6 to 8

Sitting around the table

after dinner

The first snow of winter

Anticipating Christmas

QUICK WASSAIL

Wassail, the traditional accompaniment to holiday caroling and festivity, is usually brewed in a big kettle, but here's a way to fix a few cups in a few minutes whenever the holiday spirit moves you.

½ teaspoon ground cloves
½ teaspoon ground cinnamon
¼ teaspoon ground allspice
Grated rind of 1 small orange
1 quart cranberry juice cocktail
1 quart clear apple cider
10 cinnamon sticks
10 orange slices

Place a filter in the basket of an electric drip coffee maker and add the spices and orange rind. Fill the reservoir of the coffee maker with the juices; turn on the machine. (This can also be made in a nonautomatic drip coffeepot or regular or electric percolator.) When brewed, serve in mugs, each garnished with a cinnamon stick and an orange slice.

NOTE: Before making coffee again in the coffee maker, rinse the water reservoir well and run clear water through a complete brewing cycle.

Makes ten 6-ounce servings

*C*hristmas lights everywhere

Bringing home the Christmas tree

∽

Believing in Santa Claus

∽

The smell of Christmas cookies baking

SUGAR-ALMOND CHRISTMAS COOKIES

½ cup (1 stick) butter, softened
¾ cup sugar
1 large egg
4 teaspoons milk
1 teaspoon almond extract
1 teaspoon vanilla extract
1 ¼ cups flour
¼ teaspoon baking powder
¼ teaspoon salt
¾ cup very finely chopped
   almonds
Colored sugars, sprinkles,
   jimmies, etc., for decorating

1. In a large mixing bowl, cream together the butter and sugar. Beat in the egg and milk, then beat in the almond extract and the vanilla. In a separate bowl combine the flour, baking powder, and salt, then gradually add the dry mixture to the wet mixture, mixing well after each addition. Add the almonds and mix well.

2. Roll the dough into a ball, wrap with wax paper or plastic wrap, and chill for 1 hour. Preheat the oven to 375°F.

3. On a floured work surface, roll the dough out into a circle ⅛ inch thick. Use a variety of cookie cutters to cut out different shapes and decorate with colored sugars and sprinkles.

4. Bake the cookies on a nonstick baking sheet until the edges are lightly browned, 8 to 10 minutes. Remove the cookies to wire racks to cool, then store in tightly covered containers in a cool place.

Makes 2 to 3 dozen, depending on the size of the cutters

Sending and receiving
Christmas cards

~

Feeling the joyous spirit that we all share
during the holidays

~

Coming home

~